AAMNA KHOKHAR

Be Melting Snow

A short guide on how to wash yourself, of yourself.

First published by Mental Health Publishing 2022

Copyright © 2022 by Aamna Khokhar

All rights reserved. No part of this publication may be reproduced, stored or transmitted in any form or by any means, electronic, mechanical, photocopying, recording, scanning, or otherwise without written permission from the publisher. It is illegal to copy this book, post it to a website, or distribute it by any other means without permission.

Aamna Khokhar has no responsibility for the persistence or accuracy of URLs for external or third-party Internet Websites referred to in this publication and does not guarantee that any content on such Websites is, or will remain, accurate or appropriate.

First edition

Cover art by Adam Saxby
Editing by Mohammed Imran
Illustration by Aamna Khokhar

This book was professionally typeset on Reedsy.
Find out more at reedsy.com

Contents

Preface		iv
Illustrations		vi
1	New Beginnings	1
2	Love, Love, Love.	8
3	Choose Your Path	15
4	Dreams do come true	20
5	"I am as my bondsman thinks of Me"	26
6	Fears	32
7	Letting Go	38
8	Forgiveness	44
9	Accepting your Dark Side	51
10	Interdependence	57
11	Festive Seasons	63
Aamna Khokhar in her own words		68
A bit more about Leaf Coaching		69
Reader Notes		70

Preface

This is the first edition of 'Be Melting Snow'. This phrase is taken from a translation of Jalal-uddin Rumi's poem. In his poem he says, '*Be melting snow. Wash yourself, of yourself.*[1]' Rumi is the alchemist of the heart *par excellence,* he is revered as one of the best poets of all time, and encapsulates timeless themes with erudition, but more importantly, with the sense that he knows the human soul intimately well. In this book, Aamna Khokhar is trying to help people with oft recurring themes in our lives such as fear, forgiveness and letting go. Aamna pays homage to the great Anatolian poet through having the book's title to be an excerpt from one of his Ghazals, in honour of the power of Rumi's transformative poetry.

The phrase, '*Be Melting Snow: Wash yourself, of yourself*', sets the lens through which Aamna would like readers to read this book. Be open to having your heart melt as you meander through the chapters. Take time to read each quotation. Aamna's humble aim is for this book to be part of the *tazkiyah*[2] genre Muslim writers have been writing since the early days of Islam. In that sense, Rumi's instruction to '*wash yourself, of yourself*' is rather apt.

---

[1] Coleman Barks, *The Essential Rumi.*

[2] **Tazkiyah** is an Arabic-Islamic term alluding to "*tazkiyat al-nafs*" meaning "sanctification" or "purification of the self".

Whilst this book isn't written just for Muslims, it references the Qur'an and other religious texts, as, I believe, these texts are there for a universal self-development as much as they are for guiding a faith-community through the daily travails of life.

To get directly in touch with Aamna to find out more about faith-sensitive life coaching please email info@leafcoaching.com.

Mohammed Imran, March 2022

Illustrations

The illustrations in this book have been all created by Aamna Khokhar. They are there to lead readers into a more contemplative space when they go through the book, especially as, at times, the content can be rather heavy, and bring up some uncomfortable feelings. The illustrations are designed to help people refocus on the heart of the matter, and can be used as a place to contemplate what the water colour painting represents. Each illustration has an accompanying meditation/reflection, and every painting was created specifically for the chapter it is featured in.

1

New Beginnings

"He is the Originator of the Heavens and the Earth! When He decrees a matter, He simply tells it, "Be!" And it is!"[3]

A New Year a New You.

What would it be like to be able to create a new you? On any day of your choosing, at any point in time you can choose again who you want to be. You can make resolutions, change your habits or simply rewrite scripts to old relationships. You can surprise yourself and others with a brand new you! That's what new beginnings are all about!

The creation of a new and reenergised life lies in understanding the inter-relationship between our unexamined thoughts, words and actions, and how through a structured and consistent

---

[3] The Qur'an, surah Baqarah (The Cow) verse 117. The Clear Quran, Dr. Mustafa Khattab

critical evaluation of these three key areas – we can come to create ourselves anew. We create our context through our words and action, and these in turn come from the beliefs we have. The beliefs we have come from many places, but how often do we take stock and think about whether these beliefs are really from our own making, or have they been handed down to us - or even worse - have we just been conditioned into them.

> *When it is said to them, "Follow what Allah has revealed," they reply, "No! We only follow what we found our forefathers practicing." Would they still do so, even if their forefathers had absolutely no understanding or guidance?*[4]

One way of reflecting and evaluating is to go deep into your thoughts and think about who you want to be and what you would like to create in your life. Be free in your consideration of the different areas in your life and when choosing, pick something you really want to be working on. Don't be afraid of being confronted by it. It helps to be totally honest with yourself and remember that you are doing this just for yourself and no one else.

* * *

---

[4] The Clear Quran, Dr. Mustafa Khattab (Qur'an 2:170)

Reflection: 'The final result is in His hands, start your flight. Even with wet wings, attempt your take off.' [translation of an Urdu poem].

* * *

Creating a New You

There are many reasons why people create and stick to habits. To stick to the changes you want to make you must consider your *intentions* and not the *results* you are trying to achieve. Let's take weight loss as an example; instead of saying 'I want to lose 5kg' which will have you focusing on the result you can focus instead on *why* you want to do that. The reason might be that you want to be healthier and revitalised. So a more effective intention is '*To be healthy and full of vitality*'. With the former scenario you are actually focused on the very thing you don't want, which according to the '*law of attraction*'[5] could actually bring about more of what you are trying to avoid. Alternatively, focusing on your intention, can actualise the intended outcomes (which is more important than the specific process or course of action).[6]

Focused on the intention it's easier to create a desired outcome 'I want to be able to run a mile with ease'. From such an outcome you will create better actions, you are more likely to find out

---

[5] You can read more about the Law of Attraction here: https://www.thelawofa ttraction.com/what-is-the-law-of-attraction/. Please note that this isn't an endorsement of the law of attraction as such, however, I do find it helpful to signpost to various personal development theories, especially when the relate directly to the subject matter at hand.

[6] This isn't to say that procedural matters, project planning and SMART objectives (read here: https://www.professionalacademy.com/blogs-an d-advice/what-are-smart-objectives-and-how-do-i-apply-them) are not important. They very much are. What I am trying to say is that these are all tools for you to use in your quest to achieve x or y goal. The real matter at hand is your motivation and why you are planning a certain course of action in your life. It is the why first, and then the how. Otherwise you will go down the rabbit hole of procedural nit-picking if and when things go awry.

what it takes to live a healthier lifestyle, eating the right kinds of foods and engaging in the right kinds of exercises, that, in turn, will cause the weight to drop off and stay off.

How To Frame Your New Habits

To achieve what we want we must clearly define it. In the following steps I will guide you through how to correctly formulate your habits:

- Create an intention that is in alignment with your values[7] and the kind of life you would like to live. Be inspired by it.

- Define what you want as an outcome, remember this is not about stating what you don't want but rather shaping what it is that you do want. This should be what you would get if you fulfilled your intention.

- Create an action plan with tasks that will bring you to your desired outcomes. This way consistent small steps, will lead

---

[7] In the bestselling book, The Chimp Paradox, Prof Steve Peters talks about the 'Stone of Life'. You can read a synopsis here, and this will help you formulate your own values and your guiding principles of life, if you haven't done work around this previously. https://cashflowcop.com/my-stone-of-life/

to you achieving your desired long term goals.

- Create a timetable where you map the things that you are doing on a day-to-day basis, look at those activities and decide which of those are serving you and which do not. Those that are superfluous, ineffective or not part of a greater purpose can be removed.

- In the same timetable add your new activities that serve the greater purpose.

- Create rewards for yourself when you fulfil your intentions through your chosen activities and enjoy your transformation. Be patient with the results and notice what you are grateful for whilst on the journey.

- If things don't go per plan don't give up on all your efforts. Just take stock to work out why it didn't work and then keep on going.[8]

At any point in your life you can make new decisions about who you are and who you want to be, it doesn't matter who you have been, it's never too late. Be true to yourself and create a you that lives a life out of the ordinary. You deserve it.

---

[8] This step is critical, as things are more likely to fail than not, in the majority of cases. The key is to pick ourselves up, learn from our experiences and to adjust any of the previous steps to take into account the learning we have just made. That way, the 4th or 5th time you try, it will work. It is important that you acknowledge that this isn't related to your own lack of willpower, and that it is a failing on your part personally. It can take anywhere from 18 to **254 days** for a person to form a new habit and an average of **66 days** for a new behaviour to become automatic, according to this Healthline blog: https://www.healthline.com/health/how-long-does-it-take-to-form-a-habit#takeaway

2

Love, Love, Love.

'The Prophet Muhammad, peace and blessings be upon him, said: "The souls are (like) an army joined (in the world of spirits) whichever souls knew each other (in that world) are attracted towards each other (in this world) and whichever remained distant and indifferent (there) are disinterested to each other (in this world)"'[9]

'And it is among His signs that He has created for you wives from among yourselves, so that you may find tranquillity in them, and He has created love and kindness between you. Surely in this there are signs for a people who reflect.'[10]

---

[9] (Saheeh al-Bukhaari, Kitaab Ahaadeeth al-Anbiyaa', Baab al-Arwaah junood mujannadah).

[10] Surah Ar-Rum, verse 21. Translated by Mufti Taqi Usmani

Love, Love, Love.

Love is such an elusive thing, there seems to be an art to loving relationships. Some of us get it and others, well, we just don't. If you're in search of the one or if you have already found them, it's important to realise that you *are* in control, and genuine love is not such an elusive thing.

We often think we are alone in our experience of love, that the plight we may suffer is ours alone, that others are very much in control and living powerfully. However, if we look a little deeper, we find that we all experience the same joys and sorrows, the same gains and losses: in relationships we are all, in fact, in the same boat. Men and women all experience the same emotions in relationships, we are often so focused on the differences between us we forget how similar we are. The key to transforming our experience of love is to understand *yourself* first and then to share that with *others* around you – and in the process identify commonalities.

* * *

Reflection: Truly the most powerful force. One that can move mountains off our shoulders, change the contours of our hearts, soften the tongue, change the course of life.

* * *

We often think that love emanates from our partner. Be that in the way they treat us, or how we *perceive* they feel about us. We believe that if a partner is treating us well, then that must mean there *is* love. If, on the contrary, there is an absence of those displays of affection, then that must mean there is *no* love. If we shift our focus for a moment, we can see that love actually emanates from within each of us. We are the ones who have the power to generate love in our lives. When we feel unloved and disconnected, it can be something that is happening within our own cognitive state of mind, and not located outside in another person. So in order to feel love and connection, we must be brave and generate that from within *ourselves* first and foremost. The love that we get from others is a bonus. The actual work is to be someone who generates loves for yourself first and then also for others.

> *"The Day when neither wealth nor children will be of any benefit. Only those who come before Allah with a pure heart will be saved."*[11]

We often feel that if we give away too much love, give away too much of ourselves, then we may, in some sense, have less love available for ourselves, and thus many of us often have a scarcity mindset for loving. However, this could not be farther from the truth. Love has no measurable end, there is no way of running out of love. The universe has an amazing way of looking after us, when you give in abundance you also receive in abundance.

---

[11] Qur'an, surah Ash-Shu'ara, verses 88-89.

The love we give away comes back to find us. The more love you choose to give away, the more love you will have. It is precisely when you withhold love that you often find that you *feel* unloved. So give away your love and watch it return manifold.

> 'Abu Huraira reported: The Messenger of Allah, peace and blessings be upon him, said, "You will not enter Paradise until you have faith and you will not have faith until you love each other. Shall I show you something that, if you did, you would love each other? Spread peace between yourselves."[12]

In the section below, I have shared some practical tips to help implement these ideas in your own life.

- Show interest – If your partner is telling you something they are interested in, be interested in it, even if it is not your thing. Encourage your partner to discuss the things they find interesting this will make them feel loved and regarded for who they are. Extend this across their joys and their sorrows and do this from the get go.

- Be the person you wish to see in a relationship – Ask your partner what you can do to make them happy instead of

---

[12] Sahih Muslim. Grade: '*sahih*'

looking at what they do for you. Assess your effectiveness as a partner as opposed to assessing theirs.

- Be happy for your partner – if your partner has an outstanding success, be happy for them. Be a sponsor for their growth and development. It's better to have two people bettering each other than two people tearing each other down because of insecurities.

- Be open and honest about all things – Talk to your partner about the things you think and feel, sharing vulnerabilities and asking your partner to do the same will build trust and honesty in your relationship.

- 'Fight' kindly – if you disagree on something, be mindful that the intention of the fight is not to hurt the other person but just to share your concern. Manipulating your partner in guilt/anger or stories from the past is likely to lead into a power struggle which no one ever wins. Be honest about what hurts and be responsible for your own feelings.

- Touch often – hold hands and welcome each other into your space, it builds affection. A practical exercise for you to try with your partner. Look into your partner's eyes for three minutes without looking away or giggling. See yourself in their eyes, see their vulnerability and see their love.

'Your Lord says, 'Call on Me and I will answer you'[13]

---

[13] Qur'an. Surah Ghafir, verse 60.

3

Choose Your Path

"... and [we have] created you in pairs"[14]

There are an increasing number of us out there who are looking for love and maybe feeling quite stuck. What was different during the times of generations passed?[15] When did finding a partner or looking for love become such an impossible task?

A friend of mine recently sent me a quote and it went something along the lines of 'treat your wife the way you would want your daughter to be treated', I thought that was sweet and a nice reminder for the men folk. What followed was a question for me "Would a woman treat a man the same way?" It got me thinking, and 'I don't know' was the honest answer. What it did make me wonder was why we are so concerned with what we will get in a relationship, rather than what we give? Why do

---

[14] Qur'an Surah 78, Verse 8

[15] Not that matchmaking in previous generations was issue free.

we have a long list of what we want in a relationship, but have never written one looking at what we have to give in? We think deeply about who we would like to marry, but do we consider who we are in the context of a relationship? Maybe we are afraid of being manipulated or hurt, but in such circumstances, we have a choice to leave. Byrne and Clore[16] (1974) suggest that people are motivated by the positive stimuli that they receive in a relationship, so when we make a list of wants we would like to receive, they should be matched with a list of qualities we have to give, so that we are likely to sustain a long term and satisfying relationship. If during courtship, and in the pursuit of finding a partner, we concern ourselves with *giving* rather than getting, we can focus on our nature and traits rather than the opposite.

* * *

---

[16] A Reinforcement-Affect Model of attraction, https://www.researchgate.net/publication/279431465_A_Reinforcement-Affect_Model_of_Attraction

Reflection: Salaah, dua, dhikr, reverence. He is on the straight way, you will find Him there.

* * *

How do we decide whom we should consider for marriage? In this world of web 2.0, we oftentimes have a transactional and, dare I say, superficial approach to matchmaking; our approach can be judgemental in nature, that is based on one or two pieces of limited information. With the advent of matrimonial websites and apps, we have many potential options at our finger tips and that often leads to the misconception that we have a great deal of choice. With this plethora of seemingly unlimited choices, we can become obsessive about looks, professions, and even hobbies. However, Caspi and Herbner[17] (1990) found that those with more similarities tended to be happier when they were married. So if the old adage, 'opposites attract' isn't necessarily true, then our potential pool of partners - where there is a chance of long term happiness - is probably smaller then we think. In turn, then, to be successful in finding such a person, it becomes paramount that we know ourselves first and foremost. For that allows us to be clearer on what it is that we are looking for.

'Whoever knows himself, knows his Lord'[18]

When we are trying to get married it is easy to focus on others and trying to establish whether or not they are the one. In this process, we can often overlook ourselves, to see whether or not we too have the desired qualities sought after in a spouse. Sometimes we find ourselves being attracted to a litany of unsuitable characters, without really understanding why. Initially the person could seem like the ideal person, and yet soon we discover they are anything but ideal. To truly

---

[17] **Continuity and change: Assortative marriage and the consistency of personality in adulthood.** https://psycnet.apa.org/record/1990-14647-001

[18] Quoted in *Kemyaye-e-sa'adat* by Imam Ghazali as an aphorism.

understand this phenomenon, consider this: who we *are* in the world, in turn, attracts the characters that come along. Thus it is in our control (through our thoughts, words and deeds) to attract the people in our lives, including a spouse. For example, if I am generous and happy then I am likely to meet someone who is the same as me, however, if I am generous but not really happy with that trait then it could be that I will meet someone frugal. It is paramount before entering a relationship that we consider two aspects of our own selves: 1) who we are and 2) what we are projecting out into the world. These two components together make up our projection of our self to the world.

Choose your path, by knowing your own path, and then rejoice in it. To find the dream spouse we must become one. For example, if we want someone kind and generous, we too must take on those qualities, so that we might attract those in a partner. Most importantly, one must be ready to love, and be loved. In the words of Rumi,

> *"Your task is not to seek for love, but merely to seek and find barriers that you have built against it".*

4

Dreams do come true

"But no! Allah is your Guardian, and He is the best Helper."[19]

What do you dream of? Starting a business? Finding the love of your life? Do you want to have a baby? Go on a cruise? What is it that you *really* wish for? Do <u>you</u> believe you will achieve your dream?

Have you ever wanted something so bad that the desire for it burns through your body, the frustration of not having it eats you up, and the mere mention of it sends you reeling? You try to forget it and you try to divert your attention away but it's still there; your wish, your desire, your dream, and it's still waiting to come true.

This is often the lived reality of so many people. In this brief chapter we will discuss methods for actualizing and realizing our dreams.

* * *

---

[19] Surah 3: 150, The Clear Qur'an, Translated by Dr Mustafa Khattab

Reflection: Allah (SWT) opens doors from where we cannot imagine. All we need to do is ask.

* * *

How do we make our dreams come true?

Napoleon Hill wrote his magnum opus, '*Think and grow rich*', in 1937. Published during the Great Depression in the United States, Business Week magazine's *Best-Seller List* ranked it the sixth best-selling paperback business book, 70 years after it was published. In this famous work, there are a number of visualisation techniques, that together make up a process through which dreams can be realized.

Being Crystal Clear

I will categorize the initial part of this process (being crystal clear about your dream) into the following five steps:

- Ask yourself, *how much do you really want it?* Answer honestly whether you really want it, and if so, how much you want it. Picture yourself having achieved the goal, and then carry out a thought experiment of what you stand to gain if you do achieve it, and what you forfeit if you don't?

- *Why do you want it?* Is it your dream, or someone else's? Is it a societal imposition, or is it really something you want for yourself. Ask yourself why, and be honest with yourself, this is a private conversation in your head so you can say anything you like and it will be your secret.

- *What are you willing to give up* to achieve it? Decide what you would be willing to give up to have your dream come true. How much time/money/resources would you invest? Be realistic about the potential sacrifices and then consider if it is still as desirable.

- *Is it in line with your values?* What do you value most in life? Abundance, compassion, freedom, strength? Consider what your values might be, make a list of your top 5 values and consider whether your dream fits in with these. It is much more likely to come true if it does because it will be true to you.

- *What will you achieve?* Go back to the picture of you having achieved that dream and think about all that it gives you. If your heart lights up at the thought of it, then you owe it to *yourself* to give yourself the best possible chance to make that dream come true.

Execution

So let's suppose you have found that dream and you are clear on what you want? What's next? Not much is done without creating a plan; so take steps towards understanding exactly how you will achieve your goal. For example you could make a list of specific objectives (ideally SMART[20] objectives) that would lead you to your goal. It can often take longer than we envisage to achieve our dreams, and the route can be circuitous, but with perseverance and determination, you can succeed.

So now what? Let's assume that you discovered your dream, and executed a plan as best you could, now what? How long does it take the dream to manifest? What if it hasn't happened? This is when its usually time to exercise three major muscles: humility, patience and gratitude.

Once you have played your part, entrust your dreams to God. Your job is to dream, and then to try to make it a reality. Beyond that; have faith, let go, be patient, and grateful. Sometimes in this period of waiting we can get frustrated or question whether we deserve it at all. Sometimes we bargain with God.[21]

In a Prophetic tradition it is narrated that '"*Verily, Allah does not look at your appearance or wealth, but rather He looks at your hearts and actions.*"[22] As a result it's clear that it's not about the superficial elements, but rather our intentions - this is the true core and soul of an action. The result is in the hands of God, and we simply create actions and focus on the intentions behind them. Beyond this, we are asked to have faith and let go. Our role is to take out all ego and self-judgment whilst discovering

---

[20] SMART is an acronym (you can read more here: https://www.clearreview.com/resources/guides/which-smart-objectives-definition-should-i-use/) which specifies the best type of objectives that lend themselves to being executed well. S = Specific and Stretching; M = Measurable; A = Achievable and Agreed; R = Relevant; T = Time-bound.

[21] Exercising patience and gratitude earns us Allah's favour. In the Qur'an *patience* is mentioned 90 times. God also tells us that if we are grateful he will give us more. Surah Ibrahim, verse 7.

[22] Source: Ṣaḥīḥ Muslim 2564; Grade: **Sahih** (authentic) according to Muslim

our goal, and then to remove all self-limiting beliefs when we execute. Finally we need a quiet confidence, and a silent knowing that God loves us, no matter what. And that dreams *do* come true and yours can too.

5

"I am as my bondsman thinks of Me"

'I am as My bondsman thinks of Me. I am with him when he makes mention of Me. If he makes mention of Me to himself, I make mention of him to Myself; and if he makes mention of Me in an assembly, I make mention of him in an assemble better than it. And if he draws near to Me an arm's length, I draw near to him a fathom's length. And if he comes to Me walking, I go to him at speed.'[23]

There is a notion, expressed in various faiths and belief systems that our thoughts themselves influence the world around us. In Islam, it can be best expressed by the above Hadith Qudsi, that describes how God reciprocates

---

[23] A Hadith Qudsi of the Prophet Muhammad (pbuh). A Hadith Qudsi (or Sacred Hadith) are so named because, unlike the majority of Hadith which are Prophetic Hadith, their authority (Sanad) is traced back not to the Prophet but to the Almighty. This particular narration can be found in the following books: Narrated by Abu Huraira, and collected in the books of al-Bukhari, Muslim, al-Tirmidhi and Ibn Majah.

based on our own thoughts and actions. Another term which first appeared in the West in the late 19th Century is called the 'Law of Attraction', and this term was quickly co-opted by the New Thought spiritual movement[24]. However, it is a term that, with some adjustments, can be traced back millennia. For example, the notion that we attract what we think about and that our minds have the power to manifest our thoughts into reality has parallels in Buddhism.

I wanted to briefly expand upon the essence of this idea, as I see it, which is that *we attract what we predominantly think about*. As such, controlling what we think about is very important so that we focus on what we are looking for in our lives, and not the opposite.

By focusing on the positive thoughts, we bring positive experiences into our lives and vice versa.

* * *

---

[24] Prentice Mulford, in the chapter entitled 'The Law of Success' in '*Your Forces and How to Use Them*': https://archive.org/details/yourforcesandhoo9mulfg oog?view=theater#page/n66/mode/2up

Reflection: Allah (SWT) is Love, and if you believe He loves you, then even in the darkest of night you will feel his light shine through for you.

* * *

Let us look at the practical application of this notion that *we create the world around us through our thoughts and intentions*, specifically in the domain of financial independence.

Many people strive to achieve financial independence, with some people succeeding, and others falling short of their intended goal. Let's stop and think what is it that makes some people reach their goals whereas others do not? Jack Canfield wrote the famous book 'Chicken Soup for the Soul'. His journey begins with him sticking money on his ceiling above his head so that every day when he woke up he would see this material reminder of abundance. After a certain amount of time, he sent a book he had written to a publisher. It become a success, and before long Jack had amassed a small fortune. In his book he describes how he visualized his success, remaining steadfast in his journey of attracting abundance, and then after all this, went with the flow.

Another way of using this notion of *cosmic and universal reciprocity*, is to use this principle in building and forming relationships. For example, if we focus on the positive aspects of a person's characteristics then this will certainly lead us into a virtuous cycle of seeing even more positive characteristics. Visualizing yourself in a great relationship, for example, if you're not married and would like to find your life partner, could be just the tool to help unblock this aspect of your life, just as Jack Canfield did in his life.

Creating this positivity in your life could be developed in the following method:

- *Firstly* what you want must be a well-defined and clear thought. If it's good health you want to achieve, then be clear on what that specifically looks like. Maybe you want a complete change of your diet, one that will bring you optimum health. Outline exactly what that that means and when it should be done by.

- *Secondly* this must be followed by a strong belief that it <u>will</u> happen. Here you need your faith to kick in. if you say you want optimum health and think it will never happen[25], then it will never happen. So add faith and belief to your ask.

- *Thirdly* Rhonda Byrne[26] adds that we must add emotions to this, so when you are designing this new diet and its impact on you, really feel the positive emotions that will come with it.

- *Fourthly* we must also visualize clearly what we want to achieve. Use all of the senses to describe this new diet, how it makes you feel and the impact it has on your health and well-being.

---

[25] See this article about self-fulfilling prophecies https://positivepsychology.com/self-fulfilling-prophecy/

[26] https://baos.pub/5-lessons-from-the-secret-series-by-rhonda-byrne-bec1b5133855

- *Fifthly* its more likely to happen if we imagine it as though it is already happening (or in some ways it has already happened). So we may express our gratitude for it having come into existence already.

All this will lead to actions that are in harmony with the thoughts that you are having and the more you do this the more naturally it will flow.

How can you get started with this? Well, gratitude attracts abundance[27] so why not sit and think about what you're grateful for in your life[28]. Once you are in that beautiful positive space you can begin the process of attracting into your life all that you love and desire.

---

[27] Qur'an 14:7: And ⌜remember⌝ when your Lord proclaimed, 'If you are grateful, I will certainly give you more.

[28] Gratitude jars are a great idea. For more on this please see: https://www.milanomonuments.com/blog/how-to-practice-gratitude-with-a-jar-full-of-thankfulness

6

Fears

> *"We will certainly test you with a touch of fear and famine and loss of property, life, and crops. Give good news to those who patiently endure— who, when faced with a disaster, say, "Surely to Allah we belong and to Him we will ⌜all⌝ return."*[29]

Fear, hunger and loss of wealth are a test to us. They are testing whether we can detach ourselves, put aside the ego and focus on patiently persevering despite the fear, hunger and loss of wealth. God promises good tidings to those who face up to challenges with patience and realise that they are simply temporary hardships and should therefore be treated as such, for 'verily after hardship comes ease' (94:6)

* * *

---

[29] 2:155-156, Qur'an (translated by Dr. Mustafa Khattab)

Reflection: Fear is a double-edged sword. It alerts us to danger. If we overcompensate it can be debilitating.

* * *

We all have something we fear. It might be fear of failure, rejection or even death. Why do we run from them instead of facing them? Why can they become so debilitating?

There are two types of fears: irrational and unhealthy fears such as the fear of a spider or obsessively being afraid that someone could die, and healthy/rational fears such as the fear of becoming ill if you smoke, and the fear of injury if faced with an uncaged lion. It is the former fears that we ought to challenge.

Often the intentions behind fears can become quite muddled and fear will present itself as quite rational and healthy. We may fear public speaking out of fear of being ridiculed and rejected; which can appear to be quite rational. However, upon closer enquiry, we will find that the fear is irrational. Although we cannot control the feelings of others we can control our own. We can choose to see that full and authentic self expression is not to be feared.

Ultimately fears are there to keep us safe. Similar to an overprotective parent, they don't want us to be hurt or ridiculed, the intention behind them is positive. As adults we can rationalise and question what the positive intention of the fear is and then negotiate with the fear to appease it[30]. If, whilst delivering a public lecture, you fear ridicule, you could prepare well so that you are well received. This allows you to own your fear as opposed to it owning you. Your development and growth can be dramatically and rapidly accelerated if you free yourself from irrational fears.

According to Buddhist belief our fear comes from delusional thinking and fearing what we cannot control. They use the analogy of a nightmare, if you are having a nightmare of being

---

[30] The book, 'Chimp Paradox' (Professor Steve Peters) is very good for helping differentiate between these different voices in our heads. https://chimpmanagement.com/books-by-professor-steve-peters/the-chimp-paradox/

chased by a wolf you will have all the psychological and bodily sensations of one reacting to that threat until you wake up and find it was simply in your mind. In the same way we often live our lives as though we are asleep. We carry fears around as though they are real and happening and yet we have a choice to be fully awake so that we can see that the fears are borne out of delusions that, with a little thought and self-control, we can appropriately manage and overcome.

Here are some ways to overcome fear, if and when you feel ready to do so.

- When feeling overwhelmed with fear you can change your context. The action of stepping out into the fresh air or taking a walk activates other parts of your brain that will challenge the weightiness of the fear and it will eventually dissipate.

- If panic has set in, then breathe through it. The thought of the fear can cause your heart and respiratory system to increase dramatically which only adds to the fear. Breathing slowly slows down your body functions and your mind will begin to read that there is no immediate danger and trigger the parasympathetic nervous system to relax you.

- Face the fear and stare right at it allowing the physical

reactions to wash over you. When you feel more comfortable, picture the worst that could happen and let that wash over you too. Your body cannot maintain a heightened state of anxiety with no real stimulus and therefore you fear will begin to diminish.

- Live a life where you set your own standards, don't try to be anyone else idea of perfection. You are less likely to struggle with the fear of rejection if your standards are realistic and set by you. Your ego will diminish as you begin to see that you no longer have to carry a false self.

- Talk to someone you trust and tell them about your fear. You will often find that saying it out loud will cause a change in perspective and telling someone else and having their feedback will also change your perspective further.

- You often cannot predict or change what life throws at you, your responsibility is not to control that, all you are responsible for is how you deal with it. The opposite of fear is often faith.[31] Have faith in yourself, that come what may, you have skilled yourself up enough to be able to handle it, and the rest is going to be your learning curve.

---

[31] Knowing that 'God tasks no soul beyond its capacity' 2:286

- When you successfully fight your fear and overcome it, reward your positive actions with a treat - buy yourself a book; make yourself your favourite sandwich or give yourself a hug.

In life we must face the fears and choose to walk bold, whilst brimming with faith, armed with a skilled, thinking mind. And a smile.

7

Letting Go

"They abandon their beds to cry unto their Lord in fear and hope, and spend of what we have bestowed on them. No soul knows what is kept hidden from them of joy, as a reward for what they used to do".[32]

"Pray when the sky is black, give alms, ask your Lord for freedom from the oppression of unwanted thoughts."[33]

What do we need to let go of? Thwarted intentions, lost loves, anger, being wronged, humiliation, shame, greed and regret? So many traps to navigate whilst walking the path to freedom.

So how do we let go? Well first we must understand the

---

[32] Qur'an 32:16

[33] Attributed to Imam Sha'fi.

mechanism of entrapment. Hawkins in his book 'Letting Go'[34] describes an interesting and intimate relationship that we have with our emotional responses to experience. He suggests that our responses to an experience usually end with suppression, expression or escape. When a crisis occurs, we may suppress our feelings consciously or subconsciously pushing our feelings away in our subconscious because we are not ready to deal with it cognitively or emotionally. The soul however, knows. Somehow, we continue to exist despite this knowledge lurking around in our subconscious. Unfortunately, this response causes maturational blocks and we begin to live a life where we are caught up in a cocktail of projection, denial and other defense mechanisms. This is the antithesis of letting go, and if we cannot accept ourselves as a whole, we cannot begin to let go of the conditioning of the past that no longer serves us.

* * *

---

[34] Letting Go: The Pathway of Surrender, David R. Hawkins

Reflection: Understand your triggers, observe yourself, observe them, know yourself, know your purpose, let be.

* * *

An alternative response is to be expressive, in the hope that we expunge, release and ultimately let go. However, we need to be specific in what we mean by 'expressive'. In our hyper-individualistic world, and with our never ending claims to freedom of expression, we may delude ourselves into thinking that through 'releasing' our feelings on social media channels all of our problems will be solved. This process of release can be a dangerous one.

In the wake of the Christchurch shooting in 2019, many had a strong emotional response to the loss of innocent lives and we have the freedom to express that in whichever way we choose. If we take a moment and consider how we might be able to ultimately let go is to consider how we might be able to let those feelings _drive positive action_. We can stop resisting the love that is underlying the pain and take action that brings out the best in us.

Sometimes we turn to escapism. This is the complete denial of feelings. We try to get busy, get high, go shopping, binge watch TV. Anything to avoid the silence and the space to be alone with our thoughts. As we avoid, avoid, avoid we become like a balloon full of air until one day, we are ready to pop. The moment we stop to face the feelings and resist fighting them, we begin to experience release and ultimately let go.

In the midst of a crisis we can often seek out a victim (usually ourselves), and look for a perpetrator (never ourselves) and we are quick to develop a narrative that describes why we have been wronged. We build up stories to support our view that we are not responsible, that we don't need to apologise, that we have suffered, and that life is not fair. There's a *pay off* to holding on and this pay off is what keeps us stuck. Accepting our role, making changes, knowing that s/he just wasn't right for us, being ok with being someone who makes mistakes, knowing death happens, getting perspective on the problem, can all be messages that help us let go and to release. Once we do this, we are able to step into the light and life is able to take us on a more beautiful journey.

These sticking points are the very things that make us human. These are the aspects of ourselves that we hide whilst on our journey to peace and enlightenment, but herein lies the bittersweet irony. To truly discover ourselves and to truly reach the pinnacle of human existence and freedom, we must first accept and then let go of the power of the darkness and the shadows. We must simply shine a light on it. Prophet Jonah had been called to do God's work, and when he refused, he fled and was met with trials, eventually finding himself in the belly of a whale. Jonah was under layers of darkness, the darkness of the night, the darkness of the sea and the darkness inside the whale. He made a prayer seeking refuge from God for his mistakes, and asked to be freed from the oppression of being in the dark.

We can use this as a metaphor. We too can find ourselves in our own layers of darkness. We can take a proactive approach and try our best to sincerely get out of the darkness and ask for help from others, shining a light on the different layers. However, its the fear that keeps us stuck. As travellers on this Earth, our ultimate goal is freedom and this freedom lies in accepting this world and all that is in it as a game. We are at the centre of it all and we are the ones who can grow and let go.[35]

In the silence of that moment and in the quiet of our minds when there is nothing left to do except letting go, we have hope of reaching the peace and freedom we so desire.

---

[35] There is a prayer from the early times of the Prophet's companions. It translates as, '*Show me the truth as truth and allow me to follow it. Show me the false as false and allow me to avoid it.*'

Allah is the Light of the heavens and the earth. His light is like a niche in which there is a lamp, the lamp is in a crystal, the crystal is like a shining star, lit from ⌜the oil of⌝ a blessed olive tree, ⌜located⌝ neither to the east nor the west, whose oil would almost glow, even without being touched by fire. Light upon light! Allah guides whoever He wills to His light. And Allah sets forth parables for humanity. For Allah has ⌜perfect⌝ knowledge of all things.[36]

---

[36] Qur'an 24: 35

8

Forgiveness

"Forgiveness Means Giving Up All Hope for a Better Past" [37]

This quote often throws some people. What does it imply? That we have to let go of the possibility of a better past. Forgiveness is about doing just that. Letting go of the idea that the past ought to have been a certain way.

We have limited life energy and this is why we need to sleep. To recover and restart another day with renewed energy. Seeing as this life energy is limited we must consider where we are spending it. Many of us spend our limited energy on the past, feeling sad and depressed abut those who wronged us, about things we ought to have done and we didn't. Some spend that energy on the future, feeling anxious about family reunions because of the people we don't like, feeling anxious about the ventures we will take on and fail at. How many of us spend that energy on now? How often do we consider what we are

---

[37] *Love Is Letting Go Of Fear*, Jerry Jampolsky

grateful for? Perhaps we can think about and reflect on our *lived reality, as it is*, right now, and to appreciate conversations without hearkening back to some idyllic story from the past, or any prediction for the future. How many of us can stop and see what there is in the here and now, and live from that rich and healthy space?

* * *

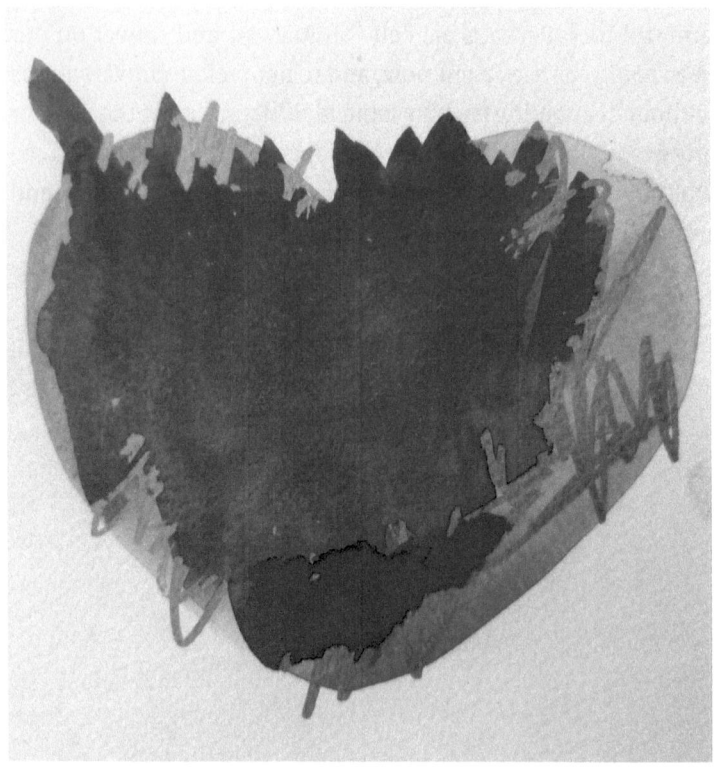

Reflection: Darkness cannot drive out darkness; only light can do that. Hate cannot drive out hate; only love can do that. Martin Luther King, Jr.

* * *

Forgiveness can release us so we are able to live from that space. It can free us from the regrets of the past and the fear of the future. Often we are reluctant to allow forgiveness in because holding on becomes a useful tool in many ways! To forgive, we must first understand what that is.

"We have not created the heavens and the earth and everything in between except for a purpose. And the Hour is certain to come, so forgive graciously."[38]

Well let's first consider what forgiveness is. It's not about who is right or wrong, or about condoning negative behavior. Forgiveness doesn't imply that there is no socially or morally acceptable behavior, but rather that we shift the focus of our mind, and reserve judgment. Forgiveness does not mean you forget the offense, but it means you align yourself back to your core purpose once more, in the knowledge that God is all-seeing. You can have had incidents in your past without actually feeling like a victim forever more. Forgiveness is not about being righteous and secretly hoping that God will one day punish the perpetrator and that you will get to watch and bask in the vindication as they suffer on account of how mean and wrong they were.

Forgiveness is about giving yourself peace of mind. It is about realizing that you are the one who is in control. You have the control to give yourself freedom from the past and to begin to live in the present. The more you forgive and let go, the more your life energy will exist in the present and not be pulled by ropes into the past nor the future. Freedom gives you your self respect back, your thoughts no longer consider how someone

---

[38] *(Quran 15:85)*

was able to make you a victim and they're no longer about the mistakes and regrets of the past. Forgiveness allows you to let go of that cosmic link between yourself and the ghosts of the past.

When we choose to forgive we can expect changes to take place and this can be confronting. We have to face the hurt and the anger and where there is hope, we will soon find that it is replaced with compassion and peace. We may have to submerge ourselves in negative feelings until they are replaced by a quiet confidence knowing you are free from the past.

Forgiveness comes in stages and is dependent upon the gravity of the situation. We have to understand what forgiveness is, to be willing to stand in the face of negative feelings and face them. To transition from being a victim to a victor, regardless of the actions of others.

If it all feels too raw you can start with an exercise that's not too triggering:

- Write out the story of what happened.

- Write out the story of what happened backwards.

- Write out the story of what happened from the middle of the incident to the end and then from the top to the middle.

- Write out the story of what happened from the middle of the incident to the beginning and then from the end to the middle.

Often when there is a perpetrator, whether it is someone else or even oneself, we dehumanize the perpetrator, through the act of name calling. It conditions us to assume that the rules of humanity and compassion cannot be extended to them/ourselves. However when we begin to consider the context in which someone behaves in a damaging way we can begin to see why they hurt us. Once we are able to get into those shoes, forgiveness is on its way.

We can choose forgiveness, compassion and letting go of resentful feelings. Above all the key is that we are *choosing* to live free of the ghosts from the past.

"And the retribution for an evil act is an evil one like it, but whoever pardons and makes reconciliation – his reward is [due] from Allah. Indeed, He does not like wrongdoers."[39]

---

[39] *(Quran 42:40)*

Reflection: It is messy, it is deep, it is raw. The antidote to the pain is forgiveness and mercy.

9

Accepting your Dark Side

"⌈Remember⌉ when your Lord said to the angels, "I am going to place a successive ⌈human⌉ authority on earth." They asked ⌈Allah⌉, "Will You place in it someone who will spread corruption there and shed blood while we glorify Your praises and proclaim Your holiness?" Allah responded, "I know what you do not know."[40]

We are taught from a very young age on how to behave, and the parameters of 'normal' behaviour are set out as part of our socialisation. We all have within us, however, the ability to deviate from these societal norms, and even those related to our own internal moral compass. The passage above, enigmatically, sets out the framework on how we should accept this dark side of ours. We are capable of the most abhorrent things, however, there is a magical and wondrous side to our nature, that is only understood in contradistinction

---

[40] Qur'an 2:30

to that dark side. God simply responds to the angels that, "I know what you do not know".

Throughout history we have been taught that we must 'kill' the dark-side, those negative characteristics and weaknesses within us. But is that even possible, without facing them? And if so, is it even healthy? What we resist persists, so if we spend all our time killing and eradicating a side of us without understanding and accepting it, are we at risk of doing more harm than good?

* * *

Reflection: A community of sinners. Loved by our Lord.

* * *

As human beings, we were created with a full range of emotional responses and desires, and this is the case for all humans. As a result they are natural and they have a function. So why do we need to hide the 'bad' ones and pretend they are not there. Sheryl Lee said, "the more we deny that we have a dark—side, the more power it has over us".

The healthiest way to live is to accept the beast within us, that way we can keep it in check. If we deny it and ignore it, it tends to slowly get out of control, and in time much more difficult to harness. It's hard to accept the dark side because we often feel afraid of the rejection that will follow, if anyone finds out about that side of us. We get busy creating a world where we are 'fine' and the problem is out there.

Avoiding our dark side can rob us of happiness, it can lead to depression and addictions because we are not truly connecting with our full selves or with other people (as we could be wearing a false mask of perfection). If we continue to live a picture-perfect life, and in the process denying a part of ourselves, we can become exhausted and lonely. When we accept the dark side it lives in harmony with the light and we lead a much more authentic and healthy life.

Fully accepting ourselves as people with dark and light sets us free, we become a more whole and complete person. The pressure to lead a 'perfect' life is gone and we are free to accept what's really there for us at each given moment of reflection. Once we are able to accept ourselves as whole, complete and perfect as we are, _and_ as we are not, we are able to do the same for others. The feeling of fully knowing ourselves and others, and being able to share those aspects of ourselves, is true intimacy and connection.

How do we know what our own dark side is? We need to listen carefully to the judgements we make about others, these are often the same judgements we make about ourselves. If we find fragility in someone annoying, then chances are that we find the same thing in ourselves annoying too, and will probably go to great lengths to hide it from others. In such circumstances, we may openly judge others and gossip about them to deflect the same weakness in ourselves.

We may experience feelings of jealousy, and ignoring or denying this feeling can lead to dysfunctional behaviour. However, if we are willing to accept that such feelings exist within us, and that they are natural, then we are free to deal with them (and manage any negative behaviours we may display as a result of these emotions). If jealousy, however, is an overriding feeling in our life, then we have to identify the reasons behind it.

If for example, we are feeling jealous of a friend who has had a great holiday with her dream partner, then the reason we are being triggered may be because we also want the same for ourselves. Instead of wishing it away from our friend, it's healthier to wish the same for ourselves and then establish ways to have the same possibly, even by asking our friend for advice on how to achieve this[41].

Once we begin to treat ourselves with compassion and not judge reactions within us that are normal and there to be understood, we are able to harness and manage that side of us. We become more authentic in our relationships. We are better able to allow that authenticity to show in others without judgement. We no longer fear rejection because we fully accept and respect ourselves for all that we are, and all that we are not. Fortunately, we are not just dark, or light, and *our real beauty lies in the harmony of both.*

---

[41] There is a wider dynamic, not discussed here, about the way in which social media amplifies these feelings of covetousness in humans due to the plethora of ways in which people now boast about their lives. This is a separate issues which is also the reason for rising anxiety amongst many people in this day and age.

"Indeed, We created humans in the best form."[42]

---

[42] Qur'an 95:4

10

Interdependence

"The Messenger of Allah, peace and blessings be upon him, said, "The parable of the believers in their affection, mercy, and compassion for each other is that of a body. When any limb aches, the whole body reacts with sleeplessness and fever."[43]

Have you decided that if you want the job done you had better do it yourself? Does this leave you feeling like you're trying to juggle life by yourself? Do you only feel connected when you read slogans telling you 'you can make it on your own'? Are you outwardly strong and independent, and secretly disconnected and lonely?

For a very long time we have told ourselves that independence is a more admirable trait than interdependence, and that we can

---

[43] Tradition of the Prophet Muhammad, as recorded in the books of al-Bukhari and Muslim.

fulfill our destinies on our own. We don't have the patience to teach people regarding our own preferences, and yet we feel we must have things the way we like them. We assume people around us are too busy to listen anyway, and that we couldn't possibly burden them with our problems or, worse still, our whims and desires. Managing careers, families, self perceptions and the need to appear happy at all times, can lead to a frustrating and lonely existence.

In the words of John Donne:

> *No man is an island,*
> *Entire of itself,*
> *Every man is a piece of the continent,*
> *A part of the main.*

What does Donne really mean? I believe he's talking about the human need for connection, and intimacy. That we are not designed to exist as an 'island', and that we need one another as resources for growth and love. Despite the focus nowadays on independence, research demonstrates that human beings are heavily influenced by, and dependent upon, positive social interactions. Our childhood experiences govern the quality of our future relationships and our ongoing exchanges shape our personalities. So despite the 'make it on our own' slogans we need meaningful positive interactions that feed our need for connection and intimacy, and they are vital to our lives and well-being.

* * *

INTERDEPENDENCE

Reflection: Codependence; then independence; then interdependence – dancing with the other whilst holding fast to the truth.

* * *

Having people around you is not the same as being known by people around you, and to be known we have to share of *ourselves*.

Often we are stopped (usually by ourselves) from opening up. Fully opening up might leave us feeling vulnerable, as we are having to unmask ourselves. However, we need to take comfort in the fact that we are all pretty much the same, we all have the same need to be heard and regarded. We are all struggling with something we need help with; joyous about another aspect of our life, and everyone has the same need to feel good about who they are. We can become resources for one another and support each other, both in terms of our respective life trajectories, as well helping each other when times are difficult.

> 'None of you [truly] believes until he loves for his brother that which he loves for himself.'[44]

If you believe being open, vulnerable and interdependent, is synonymous with being hurt then consider what led to that conditioning. Consider that who you are now is not the same person as you were then, and that you have a choice about who you would like to create meaningful connections with going forward.

An effective way of doing this is to firstly *decide* that you would like to become closer to other people, and having them in your life and for you to be in their life. Give up controlling the outcomes of your interactions and enjoy the journey. Make *authenticity* a priority and share openly of yourself and listen intently to the person sharing with you. Allow them to sponsor your life and your growth and do the same for them.

---

[44] Hadith of the Prophet Muhammad, peace and blessings be upon him, as recorded in the books of al-Bukhari and Muslim.

Steven Covey, in his magisterial work, 'The 7 Habits of Highly Effective People' talks about an individual's journey from dependence, to independence through to the highest realm – interdependence. Covey goes further to say that it is only with true interdependence that humans achieve their highest goals and ambitions. Interdependence relies upon us fulfilling the needs of others and, in turn, opening ourselves up enough to have our needs met by others.

So before we decide to open ourselves up and be vulnerable, it is useful to think about how and where we can do that, and most importantly, with whom.

Let us consider some options:

Resources I have

- List all the people who you would consider your 'continent' in Donne's terminology, i.e. those people who make you feel good when you engage with them. They might be partners, family members, friends, colleagues.

How do they contribute to my life?

- Identify how each of them contribute to your life in a positive way. Really think about this task as it might not be in ways that you expect, so be really honest.

How can I access them?

- Now consider if there are any obstacles to you accessing them, and if so what they might be, and how you will overcome those obstacles. E.g. my partner is busy with work a lot of the time, so in order to connect with him, I will invite him/her on a date where we can talk.

When will I do that?

- To give yourself the best chance of this increasing interconnectedness happening, set a clear date in your mind when you will aim to carry out any actions based on the the above enquiry.

So take off your armour and open up the channels for meaningful connections to develop. Benefit from, and provide benefit to, others; love and be loved by others; support and be supported by others; and nurture and be nourished by others. 'No man is an island, entire of itself, every man is a piece of the continent, a part of the main.'

11

Festive Seasons

"Give gifts to one another, you will love each other"[45]

In each faith tradition there is a festive season, and a period of time marked to represent joy, togetherness and celebration. For example, the three wise men brought Acceptance, Presence and Love; the Passover represents the deliverance of the Israelites from Pharaoh; and the *Eid ul-Adha* signifies the sacrifice made by Abraham. Today, these celebratory markers can also cause some festive anxiety.

* * *

---

[45] (Tradition of the Prophet Muhammad, peace and blessings be upon him, as narrated in the book of Al Mufrad).

Reflection: A global community of nearly 2 billion Muslims come together to fast and to celebrate Eid. More unites us than divides us.

* * *

The lead up to any holiday season is an exciting time full of joy and wonderment, however it can often be rather chaotic and overwhelming. We can find ourselves in a robotic state following the idealized commercial (or social media) standards to create the perfect family celebration. Not only do we need to entertain people in the home, and create a memorable experience, we are often conscious about the way we depict these moments for that all important festive Instagram post.

Oftentimes the focus is on the expensive gifts for family and friends, fabulous decorations, the hosting of a feast fit for royalty, and organizing entertainment suitable for a range of tastes and preferences. Let's consider how to manage any festive season so it is more relaxed:

- Plan ahead – It is wise to begin planning early, whether you have the mammoth task of hosting over the holiday period, or if it's just gifts that you need to buy, planning ahead can take out some of the stress and make the task more enjoyable. Be honest with yourself about what it is possible for you to do and what would be too much. In your plan include restorative activities for you and your loved ones too. Planning afternoons of relaxation where you can read, talk, take walks or have a much-needed lie in, are just as important as the shopping and cooking. These activities keep us centered and grounded which can be very important during the festive period. Often we work ourselves too hard and then are unable to enjoy the festivities and are left feeling overstretched and overwhelmed.

- Please don't try to be perfect – you don't have to create a winter wonderland at home, or a Utopian *Eid ul-Fitr* feast, and you certainly don't have to manage everything on your own. Consider where you might be able to use shortcuts and what is surplus to requirement. Once you have done that, then ask for help. Holiday seasons are about togetherness and often a great way to make guests feel more at home is by including them in some of the preparations. Let them share in the creation of a wonderful festive atmosphere and then credit them with applaud.

- Rein in the costs – holidays and celebrations should not *just* be about presents. If you're feeling the pinch discuss this openly with your family. The festive season is to demonstrate love and regard for one another and the pressure to go to extreme lengths to buy gifts should not be there. Maybe arrange a secret santa/Eid-variant instead, also encourage making gifts for one another. There are lots of ways we could still have festive fun without needing to re-mortgage our homes.

- Give give give - A great tradition is to make giving a part of the holiday season allowing one to focus on others instead of our own wants. Consider those who are less fortunate and how it might be possible for you to support them. Is there an aged neighbour who is lonely? Do you know of children in other countries/charity projects that would benefit from the money that would otherwise be spent on over-gifting? Is there somewhere you could donate your time to support people locally? This is also a great lesson for young children, so that they learn the real spirit of holiday seasons.

- Manage awkward interactions – On festive occasions we spend more time with people who we might not normally see in such proximity or for such a prolonged period of time. If you're triggered that your parents are overbearing or your siblings are passive-aggressive towards you, then you are not alone in feeling that way. In your mind's eye look at them, consider them with all their qualities and flaws and then choose them to be your family and accept them just as they are. You might find they come across differently when you do that. If you do find yourself in a pickle, then laughter is often the best medicine and great at diffusing tense situations. If you find yourself in an even bigger sticky situation then rehearsing some well versed stock phrases might come in handy, such as, "lets discuss that another time".

Refocusing on the essence and inner meaning of the particular festival we're celebrating can be a good technique to get back to basics on the purpose of festivities. What do we really need over the holiday season?

Acceptance of one another as we *are*; being present to the company that we *do* have (not some ideal we are led to desire); and to love and *be* loved in whatever form we may appear.

Aamna Khokhar in her own words

I have over 10 years of experience in the field of Psychology, Coaching and Mentoring. I use tools from Neurolinguistic Programming, Cognitive Behavioural Therapy, Perspective Taking and Effective Listening amongst many others and each client gets a tailored approach. My coaching philosophy is rooted in the Islamic principles of integrity and compassion, as well as an unwavering focus on client confidentiality. Since 2015 I have been running Leaf Coaching, through which I run individual and group coaching sessions.

I explore the purpose and direction in clients lives, focus on values and help them determine how much they are living in alignment. Spiritual development is a core part of the work I do with individuals and couples. My work with couples is focusing on building connection, improving communication and exploring ways of reaching common ground to build a positive future together.

As a life and relationship coach, I focus on supporting those people with their relationship challenges and relationship goals; coaching is provided from a non-judgmental perspective, with an understanding of the Islamic framework and context that many mainstream services often lack.

A bit more about Leaf Coaching

Leaf Coaching CIC is a Community Development organisation specialising in coaching, emotional support and empowerment programmes for BAME communities. Leaf Coaching is based in the UK and you can contact us on info@leafcoaching.com for arranging a coaching session with Aamna Khokhar. The web link for Leaf Coaching is https://leafcoaching.com/

Reader Notes

Use this brief section to write down notes to help you with your journey. This book is as much about your input, as it is about the text itself.

New Beginnings

READER NOTES

Love, Love, Love

Choose Your Path

Dreams do come true

READER NOTES

'I am as my bondsman thinks of Me'

Fears

Letting Go

Forgiveness

Accepting Your Dark Side

READER NOTES

Interdependence

Festive Seasons

www.ingramcontent.com/pod-product-compliance
Lightning Source LLC
Chambersburg PA
CBHW021449080526
44588CB00009B/757